Animal Groups

A Mob of Meerkats

by Martha E. H. Rustad

D1127040

PEBBLE

a capstone imprint

Pebble Plus is published by Pebble, a Capstone imprint, 1710 Roe Crest Drive, North Mankato, Minnesota 56003 www.mycapstone.com

Library of Congress Cataloging-in-Publication Data
Names: Rustad, Martha E. H. (Martha Elizabeth Hillman), 1975- author.
Title: A mob of meerkats / by Martha E.H. Rustad.
Description: North Mankato, Minnesota : Pebble, [2020] | Series: Animal groups | Includes bibliographical references and index. | Audience: Age 5-7. | Audience: K to Grade 3.
Identifiers: LCCN 2019003023 | ISBN 9781977109484 (library binding) | ISBN 9781977110442 (paperback) | ISBN 9781977109545 (ebook pdf)
Subjects: LCSH: Meerkat—Behavior—Juvenile literature. | Social behavior in animals—Juvenile literature.
Classification: LCC QL737.C235 R874 2020 | DDC 599.74/2156—dc23
LC record available at https://lccn.loc.gov/2019003023

Editorial Credits
Abby Colich, editor; Tracy McCabe, designer; Eric Gohl, media researcher; Kathy McColley, production assistant

Photo Credits
iStockphoto: kovaciclea, back cover (bottom), 2, background; Science Source: Robin Hoskyns, 17; Shutterstock: anetapics, 7, Breaking The Walls, 19, frerd, 9, kldy, 21, Luca Nichetti, 15, Mogens Trolle, 5, nattanan726, back cover (top), 1, Pereslavtseva Katerina, 11, S-F, 13, tratong, cover

All internet sites appearing in back matter were available and accurate when this book was sent to press.

Note to Parents and Teachers

The Animal Groups set supports national science standards related to life science. This book describes and illustrates life in a mob of meerkats. The images support early readers in understanding the text. The repetition of words and phrases helps early readers learn new words. This book also introduces early readers to subject-specific vocabulary words, which are defined in the Glossary section. Early readers may need assistance to read some words and to use the Table of Contents, Glossary, Read More, Internet Sites, Critical Thinking Questions, and Index sections of the book.

Printed and bound in China.

1654

Table of Contents

What Is a Mob?

Peep! A meerkat pops out
of its home. It's time to play
and hunt! More meerkats
follow. The meerkats live
in a group called a mob.

5

Up to 30 meerkats live
in a mob. One male and
one female lead the mob.
The leaders mate. Their young
make up most of the mob.

Mob Life

A mob lives in one area. This is its territory. Meerkats have a gland under their tail. They spread scent from the gland around the area. Other mobs smell it and stay away.

The mob digs burrows
in the ground. They make
tunnels. The tunnels connect
the burrows. The mob lives
in the burrows.

One meerkat watches out.

A predator is near!

The meerkat warns the others.

The mob goes into a burrow.

The meerkats are safe.

The mob hunts bugs and small animals. They sniff and dig for prey. They look under rocks and logs. Older meerkats teach the young how to hunt.

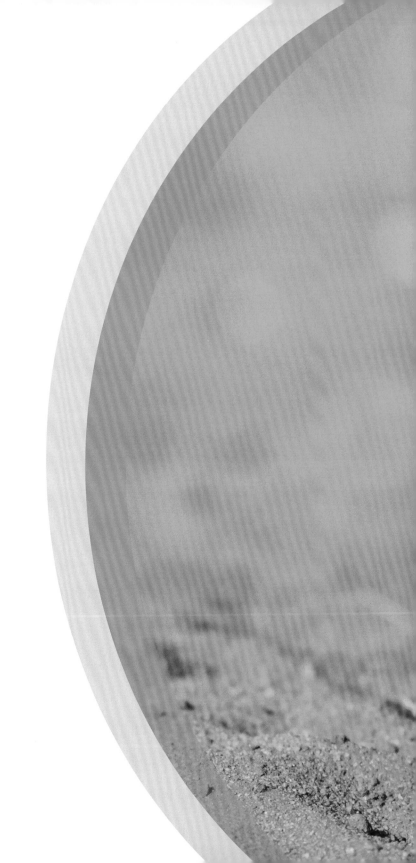

15

Pups

A female has three or four
pups at a time. The other
meerkats help care for them.
They groom their fur.
They feed them bugs.

Pups stay in the burrow
for about a month. Some grown
meerkats stay with the mob.
Some join other mobs.
Others start their own.

Meerkat Talk

Meerkats make sounds
to talk to one another. Squeal!
Danger is near! Peep! It's safe
to leave the burrow. Purr!
It's a happy meerkat.

Glossary

burrow—a hole in the ground made or used by an animal

gland—a place in a human or animal's body that produces chemicals

groom—to clean another animal's fur

mate—to join together to produce young

predator—an animal that hunts other animals for food

prey—an animal hunted by another animal for food

pup—a young meerkat

territory—the land on which an animal grazes or hunts for food and raises its young

tunnel—an underground passage

Read More

Gagne, Tammy. *Meerkats*. Animals of Africa. Lake Elmo, MN.: Focus Readers, 2018.

Monroe, Elliot. *Meerkats Work Together*. Animal Teamwork. New York: PowerKids Press, 2018.

Nelson, Penelope S. *Meerkats*. My First Animal Library. Minneapolis: Jump!, 2020.

Internet Sites

National Geographic Kids: Meerkat
https://kids.nationalgeographic.com/animals/meerkat/#meerkat-group.jpg

San Diego Zoo: Meerkat
https://animals.sandiegozoo.org/animals/meerkat

Smithsonian's National Zoo: Meerkat
https://nationalzoo.si.edu/animals/meerkat

Super-cool stuff!

Check out projects, games, and lots more at
www.capstonekids.com

Critical Thinking Questions

1. Where do meerkats live?
2. How do older meerkats help care for the young?
3. What sounds do meerkats make? What do those sounds mean?

Index